THE OFFICIAL LEEDS UNITED ANNUAL 2018

Written by Jordan Owens

Designed by Lucy Boyd

A Grange Publication

ISBN 978-1-911287-73-5

WELCOME TO THE OFFICIAL LEEDS UNITED ANNUAL 2018

As 2018 draws nearer, we hope that the next 12 months include a return to the Premier League for the Mighty Whites.

The 2016/17 season saw Leeds United narrowly miss out on a place in the Play-Offs, as the Whites recorded their highest points total in the Sky Bet Championship in ten years.

This time around, with a new owner, new head coach and arguably a stronger playing squad than last year, expectation levels around the city have risen.

In this year's Annual, we take a closer look at everyone tasked with trying to help the club back to the promised land.

We also welcome Thomas Christiansen to Leeds United; we get to know the new boss, learn about his philosophies and take a look back at his playing career.

Once you've delved deeper into the world of Leeds United, it's time to test your knowledge of the Whites with a series of quizzes and puzzles!

We hope you enjoy it.

Marching on Together!

CONTENTS

SEASON REVIEW

After the worst possible start, few would have predicted Leeds would spend the majority of the season challenging for the Play-Off places. We look back at the last campaign and pick out some of the highlights along the way...

AUGUST

DATE: SUN 7TH AUG
SKY BET CHAMPIONSHIP
Queens Park Rangers 3 (Onuoha 4, Chery pen 73, Polter 90+4)
Leeds United 0
VENUE: Loftus Road
ATTENDANCE: 16,764

LOWLIGHT

Queens Park Rangers 3-0 Leeds United

Leeds United's Sky Bet Championship campaign got off to the worst possible start on the opening day of the 2016/17 season at Loftus Road. An early goal from Nedum Onuoha gave Queens Park Rangers the lead, which was followed up by a second-half penalty from Tjaronn Chery. The win was rounded off in stoppage time by Sebastian Polter, sending Leeds straight to the bottom of the division, leaving many anticipating a relegation battle for the season ahead.

HIGHLIGHT

Sheffield Wednesday 0-2 Leeds United

Four games into the Sky Bet Championship season, Leeds United recorded a first win with an impressive victory over Sheffield Wednesday, who had been tipped for promotion after reaching the Play-Offs during the previous campaign. After going in level at the break, Marcus Antonsson's diving header gave Leeds the lead, before Chris Wood sealed the victory with a neat volley, after latching on to Kemar Roofe's cross to give the Whites a memorable win at Hillsborough.

DATE: WED 10TH AUG
EFL CUP ROUND 1
Fleetwood Town 2 (Holloway 13, Hunter 111)
Leeds United 2 (Antonsson 89, Wood pen 90+4)
(Leeds win 5-4 on penalties)
VENUE: Highbury Stadium
ATTENDANCE: 3,326

DATE: SAT 13TH AUG
SKY BET CHAMPIONSHIP
Leeds United 1 (Sacko 27)
Birmingham City 2 (Maghoma 15, Morrison 55)
VENUE: Elland Road
ATTENDANCE: 27,392

DATE: TUE 16TH AUG
SKY BET CHAMPIONSHIP
Leeds United 1 (Wood 90+3)
Fulham 1 (Cairney 77)
VENUE: Elland Road
ATTENDANCE: 21,204

DATE: SAT 20TH AUG
SKY BET CHAMPIONSHIP
Sheffield Wednesday 0
Leeds United 2 (Antonsson 63, Wood 85)
VENUE: Hillsborough
ATTENDANCE: 29,075

DATE: TUE 23RD AUG
EFL CUP ROUND 2
Luton Town 0
Leeds United 1 (Denton 23)
VENUE: Kenilworth Road
ATTENDANCE: 7,498

DATE: SAT 27TH AUG
SKY BET CHAMPIONSHIP
Nottingham Forest 3 (Kasami 16, Perquis 71, Burke 90+4)
Leeds United 1 (Phillips 83)
VENUE: City Ground
ATTENDANCE: 20,995

SEPTEMBER

HIGHLIGHT

Cardiff City 0-2 Leeds United

The Whites produced a super performance to come away with all three points against Cardiff City in the Welsh capital. In the previous season, United ended a run which had seen Cardiff unbeaten on home soil against Leeds during the last nine meetings, by recording a victory.

Like buses, along came another as the Whites recorded a 2-0 win over Cardiff in the 2016/17 season. Chris Wood's penalty gave Leeds a second-half lead, before Pablo Hernández's delightful strike wrapped up the win.

DATE: SAT 10TH SEPT
SKY BET CHAMPIONSHIP
Leeds United 0
Huddersfield Town 1 (Mooy 55)
VENUE: Elland Road
ATTENDANCE: 28,514

DATE: TUE 13TH SEPT
SKY BET CHAMPIONSHIP
Leeds United 2 (Wood 65, Bartley 86)
Blackburn Rovers 1 (Emnes 77)
VENUE: Elland Road
ATTENDANCE: 19,009

DATE: SAT 17TH SEPT
SKY BET CHAMPIONSHIP
Cardiff City 0
Leeds United 2 (Wood pen 62, Hernandez 82)
VENUE: Cardiff City Stadium
ATTENDANCE: 16,608

DATE: TUE 20TH SEPT
EFL CUP ROUND 3
Leeds United 1 (Wood 85)
Blackburn Rovers 0
VENUE: Elland Road
ATTENDANCE: 8,488

DATE: SAT 24TH SEPT
SKY BET CHAMPIONSHIP
Leeds United 1 (Wood 35)
Ipswich Town 0
VENUE: Elland Road
ATTENDANCE: 22,554

DATE: TUE 27TH SEPT
SKY BET CHAMPIONSHIP
Bristol City 1 (Pack 59)
Leeds United 0
VENUE: Ashton Gate
ATTENDANCE: 19,699

LOWLIGHT

Leeds United 0-1 Huddersfield Town

Yorkshire rivals Huddersfield Town secured a 1-0 win over the Whites, leaving United still searching for a first home win of the season at Elland Road. Australian midfielder Aaron Mooy, who was lucky to still be on the pitch after a challenge on Liam Bridcutt in the first half, saw his 25-yard effort in the second period find the top left corner. It marked the second time Huddersfield had beaten Leeds at Elland Road in 2016, after the Terriers had ran out 4-1 winners in March of the previous campaign.

OCTOBER

DATE: SAT 1ST OCT
SKY BET CHAMPIONSHIP
Leeds United 2 (Bartley 36, Hernandez 51)
Barnsley 1 (Taylor og 70)
VENUE: Elland Road
ATTENDANCE: 27,350

DATE: SAT 15TH OCT
SKY BET CHAMPIONSHIP
Derby County 1 (Russell 56)
Leeds United 0
VENUE: Pride Park
ATTENDANCE: 31,170

DATE: TUE 18TH OCT
SKY BET CHAMPIONSHIP
Leeds United 1 (Wood 29)
Wigan Athletic 1 (MacDonald 90+1)
VENUE: Elland Road
ATTENDANCE: 19,861

DATE: SAT 22ND OCT
SKY BET CHAMPIONSHIP
Wolverhampton Wanderers 0
Leeds United 1 (Silvio og 70)
VENUE: Molineux
ATTENDANCE: 23,607

HIGHLIGHT

Leeds United 2-2 Norwich City (Leeds win 3-2 on penalties)

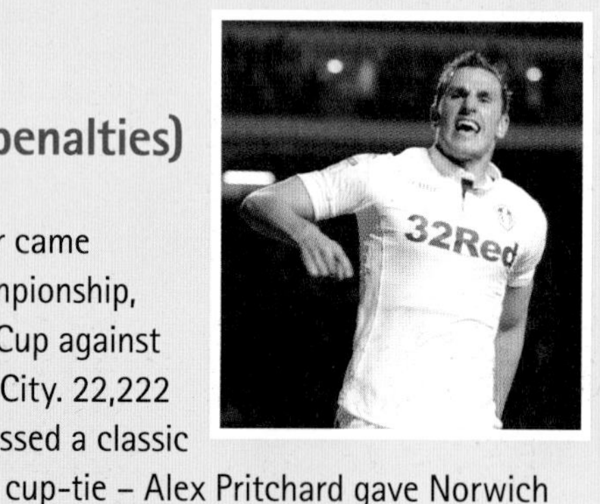

United's highlight of October came away from the Sky Bet Championship, in the EFL Cup against Norwich City. 22,222 witnessed a classic cup-tie – Alex Pritchard gave Norwich the lead inside 14 minutes, before Marcus Antonsson hit back before the break. With the scores tied after 90 minutes, the game went to extra time, but the Whites were reduced to ten men when Lewie Coyle was injured and all United's substitutes had been used. Nélson Oliveira put Norwich back in front, but Leeds hit back in the 112th minute through Chris Wood. The game then went to a penalty shootout and, after a series of saves from Marco Silvestri, Ronaldo Vieira netted the winning spot-kick to send Leeds through.

LOWLIGHT

Derby County 1-0 Leeds United

New manager syndrome occurred at Pride Park, as Steve McClaren, back in charge of Derby County, saw the Rams secure a 1-0 victory over Leeds in the first game of his return. Kyle Bartley almost gave Leeds the lead in the first half, but his header was denied by the crossbar. Johnny Russell's driving effort from the edge of the box proved to be the only goal of the match. The Whites pressed for an equaliser in the second-half, but once again were denied by the woodwork when Marcus Antonsson hit the post.

DATE: TUE 25TH OCT
EFL CUP ROUND 4
Leeds United 2 (Antonsson 43, Wood 109)
Norwich City 2 (Pritchard 14, Oliveira 99)
(Leeds win 3-2 on penalties)
VENUE: Elland Road
ATTENDANCE: 22,222

DATE: SAT 29TH OCT
SKY BET CHAMPIONSHIP
Leeds United 2 (Wood 83, Doukara 90+4)
Burton Albion 0
VENUE: Elland Road
ATTENDANCE: 24,220

NOVEMBER

HIGHLIGHT

Norwich City 2-3 Leeds United

Leeds United recorded a dramatic 3-2 victory over Norwich City in the Sky Bet Championship, following on from the EFL Cup success in October. Robbie Brady gave Norwich a first-half lead, but Pontus Jansson hit back for Leeds after the break with his first goal for the club. Chris Wood fired Leeds into the lead, but Kyle Lafferty hit back for Norwich two minutes from time. However, in stoppage time Ronaldo Vieria fired a superb winner for Leeds, giving the Whites one of the best away victories of the season.

DATE: SAT 5TH NOV
SKY BET CHAMPIONSHIP
Norwich City 2 (Brady 24, Lafferty 88)
Leeds United 3 (Jansson 57, Wood 74, Vieira 90+1)
VENUE: Carrow Road
ATTENDANCE: 26,903

DATE: SUN 20TH NOV
SKY BET CHAMPIONSHIP
Leeds United 0
Newcastle United 2 (Gayle 23, 54)
VENUE: Elland Road
ATTENDANCE: 36,002

DATE: SAT 26TH NOV
SKY BET CHAMPIONSHIP
Rotherham United 1 (Wood 86)
Leeds United 2 (Wood 14, Doukara 45+7)
VENUE: New York Stadium
ATTENDANCE: 10,513

DATE: TUE 29TH NOV
EFL CUP QUARTER-FINAL
Liverpool 2 (Origi 76, Woodburn 81)
Leeds United 0
VENUE: Anfield
ATTENDANCE: 52,012

LOWLIGHT

Leeds United 0-2 Newcastle United

League leaders Newcastle United were the only team to beat Leeds in the Sky Bet Championship in the month of October. A sold out Elland Road, with over 36,000 in attendance, saw Rafa Benitez's side run out 2-0 winners. Dwight Gayle scored a goal in either half for the Magpies, in the first league meeting between the two clubs in over ten years.

DECEMBER

DATE: SAT 3RD DEC
SKY BET CHAMPIONSHIP
Leeds United 2 (Roofe 68, Wood 90+4)
Aston Villa 0
VENUE: Elland Road
ATTENDANCE: 32,648

DATE: FRI 9TH DEC
SKY BET CHAMPIONSHIP
Brighton & Hove Albion 2 (Murray pen 23, Hemed pen 82)
Leeds United 0
VENUE: AMEX Community Stadium
ATTENDANCE: 28,206

DATE: TUE 13TH DEC
SKY BET CHAMPIONSHIP
Leeds United 2 (Wood 19, Doukara pen 90+1)
Reading 0
VENUE: Elland Road
ATTENDANCE: 21,242

DATE: SAT 17TH DEC
SKY BET CHAMPIONSHIP
Leeds United 1 (Bartley 89)
Brentford 0
VENUE: Elland Road
ATTENDANCE: 25,134

DATE: MON 26TH DEC
SKY BET CHAMPIONSHIP
Preston North End 1 (Vermijl 27)
Leeds United 4 (Roofe 17, Sacko 23, Doukara 31, Hernandez 88)
VENUE: Deepdale
ATTENDANCE: 21,255

DATE: THURS 29TH DEC
SKY BET CHAMPIONSHIP
Aston Villa 1 (Kodjia pen 86)
Leeds United 1 (Jansson 54)
VENUE: Villa Park
ATTENDANCE: 37,078

HIGHLIGHT

Preston North End 1-4 Leeds United

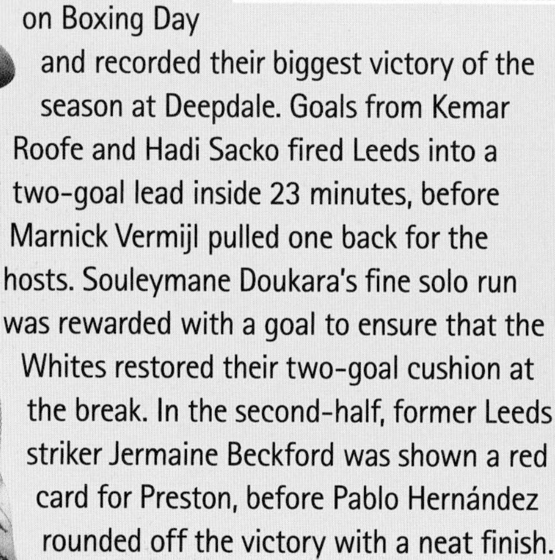

December proved to be a great month for Leeds United, with four victories and only one defeat. United travelled to Preston North End on Boxing Day and recorded their biggest victory of the season at Deepdale. Goals from Kemar Roofe and Hadi Sacko fired Leeds into a two-goal lead inside 23 minutes, before Marnick Vermijl pulled one back for the hosts. Souleymane Doukara's fine solo run was rewarded with a goal to ensure that the Whites restored their two-goal cushion at the break. In the second-half, former Leeds striker Jermaine Beckford was shown a red card for Preston, before Pablo Hernández rounded off the victory with a neat finish.

LOWLIGHT

Brighton & Hove Albion 2-0 Leeds United

United's only defeat in December came on the road at the American Express Community Stadium at the hands of Brighton & Hove Albion, who would go on to win promotion from the division. Kalvin Phillips was shown a straight red card for handballing on the line in the 23rd minute, and Glenn Murray slotted home the resulting penalty. Leeds did well with ten men, but conceded another penalty late on and Tomer Hemed this time made no mistake from 12 yards, leaving a long drive home for the travelling Leeds United support.

JANUARY

HIGHLIGHT

Leeds United 1-0 Derby County

Friday 13th is unlucky for some, but in front of the Sky Sports cameras at Elland Road, Leeds produced one of their finest performances in years defeating Derby County. The only criticism of the win was that Leeds didn't win by more. United dominated from start to finish and Chris Wood's header just before half-time secured United all three points. Former Leeds midfielder Bradley Johnson saw red late on for the Rams after picking up two yellow cards, as United showcased to the rest of the Championship that they would be challenging for a top six spot.

DATE: FRI 13TH JAN

SKY BET CHAMPIONSHIP

Leeds United 1 (Wood 45)

Derby County 0

VENUE: Elland Road

ATTENDANCE: 25,546

DATE: SAT 21ST JAN

SKY BET CHAMPIONSHIP

Barnsley 3 (Bradshaw 45, Kent 48, Hourihane 54)

Leeds United 2 (Wood 18, pen 68)

VENUE: Oakwell

ATTENDANCE: 17,817

DATE: WED 25TH JAN

SKY BET CHAMPIONSHIP

Leeds United 2 (Wood 55, Doukara 74)

Nottingham Forest 0

VENUE: Elland Road

ATTENDANCE: 24,838

DATE: SUN 29TH JAN

EMIRATES FA CUP ROUND 4

Sutton United 1

Leeds United 0

VENUE: Gander Green Lane

ATTENDANCE: 4,997

DATE: MON 2ND JAN

SKY BET CHAMPIONSHIP

Leeds United 3 (Bartley 47, Wood 66, 79)

Rotherham United 0

VENUE: Elland Road

ATTENDANCE: 33,397

DATE: MON 9TH JAN

EMIRATES FA CUP ROUND 3

Cambridge United 1 (Ikpeazu 25)

Leeds United 2 (Dallas 56, Mowatt 63)

VENUE: Abbey Stadium

ATTENDANCE: 7,973

LOWLIGHT

Sutton United 1-0 Leeds United

In our final game of the month, United were dumped out of the Emirates FA Cup by Non-League side Sutton United, in a big upset at Gander Green Lane. United fielded a much-changed side against Sutton and paid the price, being knocked out in the fourth round of the competition. The home side dominated throughout and James Collins' 53rd-minute penalty ensured their progression to the fifth round on a day to forget for the Whites.

FEBRUARY

HIGHLIGHT

Leeds United 1-0 Sheffield Wednesday

February proved to be a tricky month for the Whites, but it ended with a great victory over fellow Play-Off contenders and Yorkshire rivals Sheffield Wednesday. Leeds took a first-half lead when Chris Wood beat the offside trap and fired home Gaetano Berardi's fine cross. The Owls had a chance to equalise in the second-half when Souleymane Doukara fouled Sam Hutchinson resulting in a penalty. However, Rob Green made a super penalty save to deny Jordan Rhodes and secure Leeds a crucial three points.

LOWLIGHT

Leeds United 0-2 Cardiff City

Leeds went into February's match with Cardiff City at Elland Road on the back of six straight home wins. However, former Leeds manager Neil Warnock, now in charge of the Bluebirds, came back to haunt the Whites, guiding his side to a 2-0 victory. Goals from Sean Morrison and Kenneth Zohore gave Cardiff victory and Liam Bridcutt saw red late on for a second yellow card, rounding off a miserable day for the Whites.

DATE: WED 1ST FEB
SKY BET CHAMPIONSHIP
Blackburn Rovers 1 (Bennett 83)
Leeds United 2 (Dallas 74, Jansson 89)
VENUE: Ewood Park
ATTENDANCE: 17,026

DATE: SUN 5TH FEB
SKY BET CHAMPIONSHIP
Huddersfield Town 2 (Brown 27, Hefele 89)
Leeds United 1 (Wood 35)
VENUE: John Smith's Stadium
ATTENDANCE: 22,400

DATE: SAT 11TH FEB
SKY BET CHAMPIONSHIP
Leeds United 0
Cardiff City 2 (Morrison 53, Zohore 71)
VENUE: Elland Road
ATTENDANCE: 31,516

DATE: TUE 14TH FEB
SKY BET CHAMPIONSHIP
Leeds United 2 (Wood 27, Hernandez 47)
Bristol City 1 (Djuric 90+6)
VENUE: Elland Road
ATTENDANCE: 22,402

DATE: SAT 18TH FEB
SKY BET CHAMPIONSHIP
Ipswich Town 1 (Sears 9)
Leeds United 1 (Dallas 42)
VENUE: Portman Road
ATTENDANCE: 18,748

DATE: SAT 25TH FEB
SKY BET CHAMPIONSHIP
Leeds United 1 (Wood 24)
Sheffield Wednesday 0
VENUE: Elland Road
ATTENDANCE: 35,093

MARCH

HIGHLIGHT

Leeds United 2-0 Brighton & Hove Albion

March ended for Leeds with a fantastic win over Brighton & Hove Albion, who were occupying one of the two automatic promotion spots in the division. A double from Whites' leading goal-scorer Chris Wood wrapped up a great three points at Elland Road. Leeds took the lead when Wood headed home Charlie Taylor's cross, before adding a second from the penalty spot after Souleymane Doukara was felled in the Brighton area. The result lifted Leeds into fourth place in the Sky Bet Championship, just eight points behind second-placed Brighton.

DATE: FRI 3RD MAR
SKY BET CHAMPIONSHIP
Birmingham City 1 (Gardner 63)
Leeds United 3 (Wood 14, 67, Pedraza 81)
VENUE: St Andrew's
ATTENDANCE: 20,321

DATE: TUE 7TH MAR
SKY BET CHAMPIONSHIP
Fulham 1 (Cairney 90+5)
Leeds United 1 (Ream og 5)
VENUE: Craven Cottage
ATTENDANCE: 22,239

DATE: SAT 11TH MAR
SKY BET CHAMPIONSHIP
Leeds United 0
Queens Park Rangers 0
VENUE: Elland Road
ATTENDANCE: 30,870

DATE: SAT 18TH MAR
SKY BET CHAMPIONSHIP
Leeds United 2 (Wood 63, pen 85)
Brighton & Hove Albion 0
VENUE: Elland Road
ATTENDANCE: 29,767

LOWLIGHT

Fulham 1-1 Leeds United

Leeds travelled to Fulham full of confidence after recording a fine away victory over Birmingham City four days earlier. The Whites, without leading goal-scorer Chris Wood due to injury, took the lead inside five minutes, thanks to a freak own goal by Fulham defender Tim Ream, who sliced a clearence into his own net. Fulham pressed for an equaliser throughout the match and Neeskens Kebano was only denied by the crossbar. However at the death, Tom Cairney smashed home from 25 yards to secure Fulham a point and made the result feel like a defeat for Leeds.

APRIL

HIGHLIGHT

Newcastle United 1-1 Leeds United

After a difficult start to April, with two defeats on the road, Leeds got back to winning ways against Preston North End. Leeds travelled to St James' Park full of confidence and came away with a crucial point as the race for the Play-Offs intensified. Alfonso Pedraza saw an effort only denied by the crossbar in the first half as both teams went in level at the break.

Jamaal Lascelles gave Newcastle the lead in the 67th minute and the Magpies looked set to take all three points, however a dramatic 95th minute volley from Chris Wood sent the Leeds supporters home delighted.

DATE: SAT 1ST APR
SKY BET CHAMPIONSHIP
Reading 1 (Kermorgant 21)
Leeds United 0
VENUE: Madejski Stadium
ATTENDANCE: 23,055

DATE: TUE 4TH APR
SKY BET CHAMPIONSHIP
Brentford 2 (Sawyers 19, Vibe 34)
Leeds United 0
VENUE: Griffin Park
ATTENDANCE: 10,759

DATE: SAT 8TH APR
SKY BET CHAMPIONSHIP
Leeds United 3 (Roofe 18m Hernandez 45, Doukara 90+3)
Preston North End 0
VENUE: Elland Road
ATTENDANCE: 31,851

DATE: FRI 14TH APR
SKY BET CHAMPIONSHIP
Newcastle United 1 (Lascelles 67)
Leeds United 1 (Wood 90+5)
VENUE: St James' Park
ATTENDANCE: 52,301

DATE: MON 17TH APR
SKY BET CHAMPIONSHIP
Leeds United 0
Wolverhampton Wanderers 1 (Dicko 38)
VENUE: Elland Road
ATTENDANCE: 32,351

DATE: SAT 22ND APR
SKY BET CHAMPIONSHIP
Burton Albion 2 (Sordell 75, Kightly 77)
Leeds United 1 (Bartley 80)
VENUE: Pirelli Stadium
ATTENDANCE: 6,073

DATE: SAT 29TH APR
SKY BET CHAMPIONSHIP
Leeds United 3 (Wood 45+1, Bartley 49, Hernandez 78)
Norwich City 3 (Naismith 28, Oliveira 34, 45)
VENUE: Elland Road
ATTENDANCE: 34,292

LOWLIGHT

Burton Albion 2-1 Leeds United

Leeds United's Play-Off hopes were left all but over as the Whites slipped to a first ever defeat against Burton Albion at the Pirelli Stadium. The result all but secured Burton's Sky Bet Championship status, but left Leeds in seventh place, three points behind Fulham in sixth with two games to play.

Two second-half goals in two minutes from Marvin Sordell and Michael Kightly put Burton in pole position. Kyle Bartley hit back for Leeds and the Whites pressed for an equaliser, but the Brewers held out for the win.

MAY

DATE: SUN 7TH MAY

SKY BET CHAMPIONSHIP

Wigan Athletic 1 (Tunnicliffe 6)

Leeds United 1 (Wood pen 50)

VENUE: DW Stadium

ATTENDANCE: 15,280

With Leeds three points behind Fulham and needing a 13-goal swing to finish in sixth spot following the 3-3 draw with Norwich City in the final game of April, the clash at the DW Stadium had all but nothing riding on it, with Wigan already relegated. Leeds went behind when Ryan Tunnicliffe gave the Latics the lead. Chris Wood equalised in the second-half from the penalty spot, netting his 30th goal of the season. The Whites were unable to get a winner and finished the season in seventh spot, disappointed after spending so long in the Play-Off places, but with a lot of optimism for the 2017/18 season.

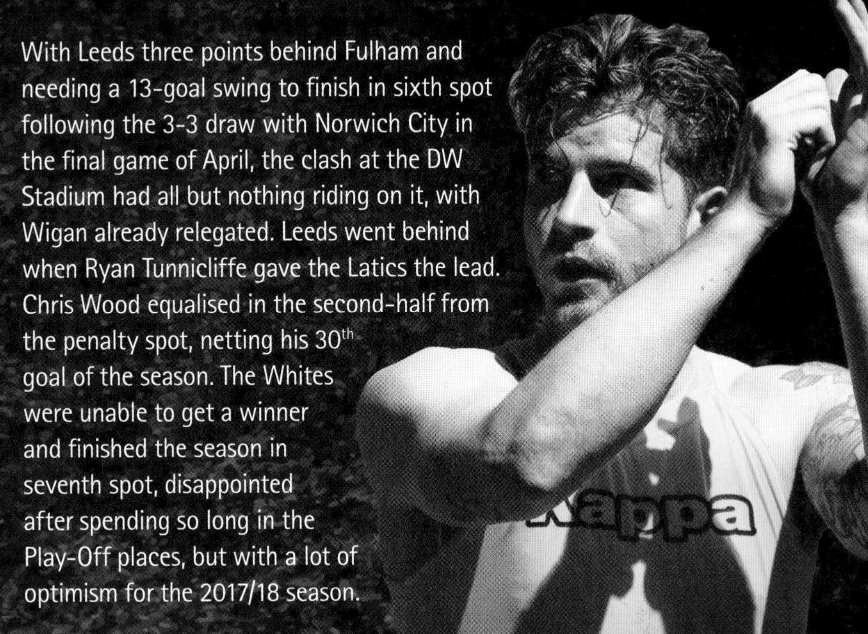

Final 2016/17 Championship table

Pos	Team	Pl	W	D	L	F	A	GD	Pts
1	Newcastle United	46	29	7	10	85	40	45	94
2	Brighton and Hove Albion	46	28	9	9	74	40	34	93
3	Reading	46	26	7	13	68	64	4	85
4	Sheffield Wednesday	46	24	9	13	60	45	15	81
5	Huddersfield Town	46	25	6	15	56	58	-2	81
6	Fulham	46	22	14	10	85	57	28	80
7	Leeds United	46	22	9	15	61	47	14	75
8	Norwich City	46	20	10	16	85	69	16	70
9	Derby County	46	18	13	15	54	50	4	67
10	Brentford	46	18	10	18	75	65	10	64
11	Preston North End	46	16	14	16	64	63	1	62
12	Cardiff City	46	17	11	18	60	61	-1	62
13	Aston Villa	46	16	14	16	47	48	-1	62
14	Barnsley	46	15	13	18	64	67	-3	58
15	Wolverhampton Wanderers	46	16	10	20	54	58	-4	58
16	Ipswich Town	46	13	16	17	48	58	-10	55
17	Bristol City	46	15	9	22	60	66	-6	54
18	Queens Park Rangers	46	15	8	23	52	66	-14	53
19	Birmingham City	46	13	14	19	45	64	-19	53
20	Burton Albion	46	13	13	20	49	63	-14	52
21	Nottingham Forest	46	14	9	23	62	72	-10	51
22	Blackburn Rovers	46	12	15	19	53	65	-12	51
23	Wigan Athletic	46	10	12	24	40	57	-17	42
24	Rotherham United	46	5	8	33	40	98	-58	23

THE WINNERS

WE TAKE A LOOK AT WHOSE PERFORMANCES WERE REWARDED WITH SILVERWARE AT THE END OF THE 2016/17 SEASON...

PLAYER OF THE YEAR
CHRIS WOOD

Striker Chris Wood topped the Official Supporters' Vote to claim the headline award following a fantastic individual campaign. Wood ended the season having netted 30 goals in all competitions for the Whites.

Wood enjoyed his most prolific return in front of goal, having made 48 appearances in all competitions for Leeds during the 2016/17 and was key in helping the Whites challenge for a Play-Off spot.

MEMBERS' PLAYER OF THE YEAR
ROB GREEN

Experienced goalkeeper and former England international Rob Green picked up the Members' Player of the Year Award after a fine season between the sticks for Leeds.

Green made a number of crucial saves throughout the season, with a major highlight being a penalty save in our fixture against Sheffield Wednesday at Elland Road.

YOUNG PLAYER OF THE YEAR
RONALDO VIEIRA

Making his debut as a substitute in the final game of the 2015/16 season against Preston North End, Vieira went on to establish himself as a key player for Leeds during the last campaign.

He made a total of 38 appearances for the Whites and scored a memorable winner against Norwich City in the league. Vieira penned a new four-year deal with Leeds in the summer of 2017.

GOAL OF THE YEAR
SOULEYMANE DOUKARA VS NOTTINGHAM FOREST

There was only one real contender for the Goal of the Year Award as Souleymane Doukara's strike against Nottingham Forest blew everything else out of the water.

Out of nowhere, the forward unleashed a thunderous volley at Elland Road which rifled into the top left corner, with many comparing it to Tony Yeboah's famous strike against Liverpool.

ACADEMY PLAYER OF THE YEAR
CALLUM NICELL

Young prospect Callum Nicell was presented with the Academy Player of the Year Award. Leeds fans keep your eye out for this potential star of the future!

PLAYERS' PLAYER OF THE YEAR
CHRIS WOOD

Chris Wood was not only named Player of the Year by his supporters, but also his team mates, in arguably one of the biggest awards to receive for a player.

Wood's ability to put the ball in the back of the net was crucial for the Whites, with his goals helping the Whites pick up three points for the majority of the campaign.

BOBBY COLLINS UNSUNG HERO
MARK BROADLEY

An award for behind-the-scenes and outstanding contribution to Leeds United, popular staff member Mark Broadley, who looks after the stadium and operations at Elland Road, was presented with the Bobby Collins Unsung Hero Award.

A NEW CHAPTER FOR LEEDS UNITED

THE SUMMER OF 2017 MARKED A HUGE CHANGE FOR LEEDS UNITED, AS NEW OWNER ANDREA RADRIZZANI COMPLETED HIS PURCHASE OF THE CLUB AND BUYOUT OF MASSIMO CELLINO.

After initially purchasing 50% of the club in December 2016, Radrizzani completed a full takeover of Leeds in May 2017.

Radrizzani is Founder and Group Chairman of Aser Group Holding, the successful Co-Founder of international sports media rights company MP & Silva and a leading figure in the sports media industry over the past two decades.

Speaking about the takeover Radrizzani said: "I am delighted to have the opportunity to become a custodian of this great football club.

"The heritage and history of Leeds United attracted me to the club and having spent time at games and at Thorp Arch, I can see that we are ready to move forward to the next level.

"This is a long-term commitment, there is a lot of hard work ahead of us and I am aware of my responsibilities as owner of Leeds United.

"I can assure all supporters that everyone at this club will be doing all we can to build a successful team at Elland Road."

Since completing his full takeover of the club, there have been many changes at Leeds United, here is what has happened so far....

NEW HEAD COACH

Radrizzani's first job was to appoint a successor to outgoing head coach Garry Monk who resigned and joined Middlesbrough. Thomas Christiansen was the man he chose; after a successful playing career the former Spanish international has had success in management in Cyprus, guiding APOEL to the First Division title in the 2016/17 campaign.

KEY APPOINTMENTS

There were new additions to the club staff at Elland Road. Angus Kinnear was appointed managing director, arriving from Premier League club West Ham, having also had previous experience with Arsenal. Victor Orta was named director of football, joining from Middlesbrough, having previously worked with Spanish outfit Sevilla.

ELLAND ROAD

Radrizzani completed the purchase of Elland Road which has been our home since 1919. The stadium is now back in the club's control for the first time since it was sold in 2004, during a period of financial difficulty. Since the purchase of the stadium, there have been many changes, with new branding around the ground, new changing rooms, new LED advertisement boards and new hospitality facilities.

NEW SIGNINGS

Thomas Christiansen's summer recruits went into double figures! The likes of Vurnon Anita joined the club from Newcastle United, whilst exciting playmakers Ezgjan Alioski and Samu Saiz joined the club from Lugano and Huesca respectively. The loan signings of young English duo Cameron Borthwick-Jackson and Matthew Pennington from Premier League sides Manchester United and Everton also bolstered Christiansen's squad.

NEW CONTRACTS

Gaetano Berardi, Liam Cooper, Lewie Coyle, Tyler Denton, Eunan O'Kane, Kalvin Phillips and Ronaldo Vieira all signed new contracts with the club, committing their long-term futures to Leeds United in the summer of 2017. The new deals ensure United's brightest prospects will be staying with the club as Leeds look to get back to the Premier League.

ANDY LONERGAN

POSITION: GOALKEEPER
NATIONALITY: ENGLISH
DATE OF BIRTH: 19/10/1983

Leeds United re-signed goalkeeper Andy Lonergan on a free transfer from Wolverhampton Wanderers in the summer of 2017. Lonergan had previously represented Leeds between 2011 and 2012 making 38 appearances before moving to Bolton Wanderers. The experienced keeper, who has almost 400 professional games under his belt, started his career with Preston North End and has also had stints at Swindon Town, Wycombe Wanderers and Fulham. Lonergan will now compete with Felix Wiedwald and Bailey Peacock-Farrell for a place in Thomas Christiansen's starting 11 during the 2017/18 campaign.

BAILEY PEACOCK-FARRELL

POSITION: GOALKEEPER
NATIONALITY: ENGLISH
DATE OF BIRTH: 29/10/1996

Bailey Peacock-Farrell found himself unexpectedly thrown into the first-team fold when he made his senior debut against Queens Park Rangers in April 2016. The Darlington-born stopper, who joined United from Middlesbrough's Academy in 2013, proved to be an able deputy, in his solitary appearance for the club and was beaten only by a late penalty in a 1-1 draw at Elland Road. Last season Peacock-Farrell continued to feature heavily for United's Under-23s and over the summer, the goalkeeper signed a new three-year contract, committing his future to the club until the end of the 2019/20 season.

FELIX WIEDWALD

POSITION: GOALKEEPER
NATIONALITY: GERMAN
DATE OF BIRTH: 15/03/1990

The German goalkeeper joined Leeds in the summer of 2017, from Bundesliga outfit Werder Bremen for an undisclosed fee, on a three-year deal. Wiedwald started his career at Bremen, before joining Bundesliga 2 outfit MSV Duisburg, where he spent two years. In the summer of 2013, he was snapped up by Eintracht Frankfurt where he spent a further two years, before re-joining his first club Werder in May 2015. Wiedwald will battle it out with Andy Lonergan and Bailey Peacock-Farrell to be United's first choice goalkeeper during the 2017/18 campaign.

VURNON ANITA

POSITION: DEFENDER
NATIONALITY: DUTCH
DATE OF BIRTH: 04/04/1989

Vurnon Anita joined Leeds United on a free transfer from Newcastle United in the summer of 2017. The versatile Dutch international who can play in midfield or at full-back, joined the Whites on the back of helping the Magpies to win promotion from the Sky Bet Championship to the Premier League, featuring 27 times during the league campaign. Anita made his breakthrough with Dutch giants Ajax, for whom he made over 100 appearances, before joining Newcastle for a fee close to £7m in 2012. Capped four times by the Netherlands, Anita will be hoping for a second successive promotion with the Whites come the end of the 2017/18 season.

LUKE AYLING

POSITION: DEFENDER
NATIONALITY: ENGLISH
DATE OF BIRTH: 25/08/1991

Full-back Luke Ayling penned a three-year deal with Leeds in the summer of 2016, joining the Whites from Sky Bet Championship rivals Bristol City. Ayling began his career at Arsenal and progressed through the ranks, before moving to Yeovil Town in 2010. Spending four years on the books at Huish Park, Ayling helped the Glovers achieve promotion from League One in 2013. He was snapped up by Bristol City the following year and helped the Robins secure a return to the Championship from League One. Ayling became United's first-choice right-back during the 2016/17 campaign, going on to make 43 appearances in all competitions.

GAETANO BERARDI

POSITION: DEFENDER
NATIONALITY: SWISS
DATE OF BIRTH: 21/08/1988

The Swiss full-back, signed for Leeds from Italian outfit Sampdoria in July 2014. Berardi, who is equally as comfortable playing on the right or the left, endured a testing start to life in English football and was sent off on his United debut, but the defender's solid performances have established him as a key figure in the side. Berardi twice won the Play-Offs during his time in Serie B – with Brescia and Sampdoria. Over the past three seasons, Berardi has been rapidly earning a cult hero status at Elland Road for his commitment to the cause.

CAMERON BORTHWICK-JACKSON

POSITION: **DEFENDER**
NATIONALITY: **ENGLISH**
DATE OF BIRTH: **02/02/1997**

Cameron Borthwick-Jackson joined Leeds United in the summer of 2017 from Premier League outfit Manchester United on a season-long loan deal. Borthwick-Jackson made his Manchester United debut against West Bromwich Albion in November 2015 and has made a total of 14 appearances for the Old Trafford side. During the 2016/17 season the full-back spent time on loan with fellow Sky Bet Championship outfit Wolverhampton Wanderers, where he made seven appearances. The defender has also represented England at various youth levels, winning caps for the Under-17s, Under-19s and Under-20s.

LIAM COOPER

POSITION: **DEFENDER**
NATIONALITY: **SCOTTISH**
DATE OF BIRTH: **30/08/1991**

The centre-back joined the club from Chesterfield in summer 2014 after catching the eye in a pre-season friendly against the Whites. Cooper, a product of Hull City's Academy, has been a regular fixture at the heart of the United defence since his arrival and his performances have led to call-ups to the senior Scotland squad. The left-sided centre-back previously spent time on loan at Carlisle United and Huddersfield Town while on the books of Hull, before earning a place in the League Two PFA Team of the Year 2013/14 as he helped Chesterfield secure promotion.

PONTUS JANSSON

POSITION: **DEFENDER**
NATIONALITY: **SWEDISH**
DATE OF BIRTH: **13/02/1991**

Swedish international defender Pontus Jansson arrived at Leeds, initially on a season-long loan from Italian outfit Torino, before the move was made permanent over the summer. The 6ft. 5in. centre-back began his career with homeland outfit Malmo FF, before moving to Torino in 2014. Jansson regularly features on the international stage for Sweden and has now reached double figures for caps earned. He became an instant fans favourite last season, due to the desire and passion shown at the heart of the Leeds defence.

MATTHEW PENNINGTON

POSITION: **DEFENDER**
NATIONALITY: **ENGLISH**
DATE OF BIRTH: **06/10/1994**

Defender Matthew Pennington joined Leeds United on a season-long loan from Premier League outfit Everton, becoming the club's 10th signing of the summer. The young defender has a wealth of experience, having had three loan spells at League One level, with Tranmere Rovers, Coventry City and Walsall. Pennington has made nine first team appearances for Everton and scored his first goal for the club in April 2017, in the Merseyside derby against Liverpool. His arrival boosts the United defence, adding further competition for places.

CONOR SHAUGHNESSY

POSITION: **DEFENDER**
NATIONALITY: **IRISH**
DATE OF BIRTH: **30/06/1993**

Young Irish defender Conor Shaughnessy is one of the latest young players to break through into the first team from the famous Leeds United Academy. Shaughnessy travelled regularly with the first team during the 2016/17 season, making the bench on a number of occasions throughout the campaign and he made his debut in United's first game of the 2017/18 campaign, coming on as a substitute in the 3-2 victory over Bolton Wanderers. The young centre-back has firmly established himself in new head coach Thomas Christiansen's first-team plans and it promises to be an exciting year for Shaughnessy.

EZGJAN ALIOSKI

POSITION: **MIDFIELDER**
NATIONALITY: **MACEDONIAN**
DATE OF BIRTH: **12/02/1992**

Leeds moved to sign Ezgjan Alioski from Swiss side Lugano for an undisclosed fee in the summer of 2017, beating off competition from several clubs for his signature. The attacking midfielder was the third highest scorer in the Swiss Super League in the 2016/17 season and at Lugano scored 17 goals in all competitions, providing 14 assists. On the international stage, Alioski is a regular starter for Macedonia and has been capped into double figures. Alioski, who has also had spells at Swiss sides Young Boys and Schaffhausen, penned a four-year deal at Elland Road.

STUART DALLAS

POSITION: MIDFIELDER
NATIONALITY: NORTHERN IRISH
DATE OF BIRTH: 19/04/1991

The Northern Ireland international soon settled into life at Elland Road following his summer 2015 move from Brentford, ending his debut campaign as United's Players' Player of the Year after being crowned by his team-mates. Dallas, who began his career with semi-professional homeland side Crusaders, earning just £70 a week, became the first United player to feature in a major tournament for 10 years when he represented his country at Euro 2016. The winger, a League One promotion winner with Brentford in 2014, made 35 appearances for the Whites during the 2016/17 campaign, scoring three goals.

PABLO HERNANDEZ

POSITION: MIDFIELDER
NATIONALITY: SPANISH
DATE OF BIRTH: 11/04/1985

Spanish attacking midfielder Pablo Hernandez joined the Whites initially on loan from Qatari side Al-Arabi, ahead of the 2016/17 season, before penning a permanent deal in January 2017. The vastly-experienced Hernandez came through the ranks at Valencia and arrived at Elland Road with over 130 La Liga appearances to his name and four full international caps. His career to date has included two spells with Valencia, sandwiching a season with fellow Spanish outfit Getafe. The 32-year-old then had a spell at Swansea, prior to moving to Al-Arabi, which also included a temporary return to his homeland with Rayo Vallecano. Hernandez signed a one-year contract extension at the end of last season, after making 38 appearances for the Whites.

MATEUSZ KLICH

POSITION: MIDFIELDER
NATIONALITY: POLISH
DATE OF BIRTH: 13/06/1990

Polish international midfielder Mateusz Klich joined Leeds United from Dutch outfit FC Twente in the summer of 2017. Starting his career at Polish outfit KS Cracovia, Klich was snapped up by German Bundesliga outfit VfL Wolfsburg in 2011. Spells at Dutch side PEC Zwolle and German outfit 1. FC Kaiserslautern followed, before moving back to the Eredivisie with FC Twente. Last season at Twente, Klich scored six goals, helping them to a seventh-placed finish and upon arriving at Elland Road signed a three-year deal for an undiclosed fee.

EUNAN O'KANE

POSITION: **MIDFIELDER**
NATIONALITY: **IRISH**
DATE OF BIRTH: **15/07/1990**

Republic of Ireland international Eunan O'Kane joined the Whites in the summer of 2016 from Premier League outfit AFC Bournemouth. The midfielder, who featured regularly in the top flight with the Cherries, spent time in Everton's Academy as a youngster before beginning his professional career with Northern Irish outfit Coleraine. O'Kane was born in Northern Ireland and represented their youth teams before opting to play for the Republic of Ireland at senior international level. He made his name in England during a two-year stint with Torquay United and was subsequently snapped up by then League One side Bournemouth in 2012, going on to make 115 appearances and helping the Cherries achieve top-flight promotion.

KALVIN PHILLIPS

POSITION: **MIDFIELDER**
NATIONALITY: **ENGLISH**
DATE OF BIRTH: **02/12/1995**

The home-grown central midfielder scored on his Elland Road debut – April 2015's 2-1 defeat to Cardiff City – just five days after making his first senior appearance away to Wolverhampton Wanderers. Phillips, who joined the club from local side Wortley Juniors in 2010, progressed through the ranks at Thorp Arch and earned a glowing reputation for his all-action displays prior to his first-team breakthrough. The youngster featured regularly in the first team for the Whites during the 2016/17 campaign, making 40 appearances in all competitions and will be looking to build on that this season.

SAMUEL SÁIZ

POSITION: **MIDFIELDER**
NATIONALITY: **SPANISH**
DATE OF BIRTH: **22/01/1991**

Exciting midfielder Samuel Sáiz signed for Leeds United on a four-year contract in the summer of 2017 for an undisclosed fee. Born in Madrid, Sáiz came through the ranks at Spanish giants Real, going on to make appearances for their B and C teams. Spells at UD Melilla, Getafe and UD Almería followed, before he was snapped up by Atlético Madrid in 2014. Sáiz then moved initially on loan to Huesca, before that move was made permanent in 2016. Last season he made 40 appearances, scoring 12 goals and provided eight assists, helping Huesca reach the Spanish Segunda División Play-Offs and the Whites beat off competition from other clubs to secure his signature.

HADI SACKO

POSITION: **MIDFIELDER**
NATIONALITY: **FRENCH**
DATE OF BIRTH: **24/03/1994**

Capped by France at Under-20s level, the pacy winger began his career with Bordeaux, but was poached by Portuguese giants Sporting Lisbon in 2014. Sacko, who also spent time on loan in his native France with Ligue 2 outfit Sochaux, joined United ahead of the 2016/17 campaign on a season-long loan deal. He made 42 appearances for the Whites last season in all competitions, scoring two goals. Sacko's deal to join Leeds was made permanent at the end of the campaign and he penned a three-year deal to remain at Elland Road.

RONALDO VIEIRA

POSITION: **MIDFIELDER**
NATIONALITY: **ENGLISH**
DATE OF BIRTH: **19/07/1998**

Born in Guinea-Bissau but having grown up in Portugal and spent time on the books of European giants Benfica, the highly-rated youngster first arrived at United on trial in 2015 after catching the eye playing for York's i2i Football Academy. Vieira, who moved to England with his family in 2011, was thrown into the spotlight during the final week of the 2015/16 season, making his senior debut away to Preston North End, just two days after signing his first professional contract. Last season, Vieira established himself in the first team and made 38 appearances in all competitions, scoring one goal. He was rewarded with a new four-year contract in the summer of 2017 and also made his international debut, helping England Under-20s win the Toulon Tournament.

CALEB EKUBAN

POSITION: **FORWARD**
NATIONALITY: **ITALIAN**
DATE OF BIRTH: **23/03/1994**

Leeds United completed the transfer of young forward Caleb Ekuban for an undisclosed fee in July 2017. The pacy forward joined the club from Italian Serie A outfit Chievo Verona, signing a four-year contract with the Whites. Having come through the ranks at Chievo, the striker has also had loan spells with fellow Italian sides FC Südtirol, AC Lumezzane and AC Renate. Last season Ekuban spent the season on loan at Albanian outfit FK Partizani, for whom he played in the UEFA Champions League and Europa League. He made 34 appearances in the Kategoria Superiore for Partizani, scoring 17 goals, as the club finished runners-up in the division.

JAY-ROY GROT

POSITION: **FORWARD**
NATIONALITY: **DUTCH**
DATE OF BIRTH: **13/03/1998**

The Whites completed the signing of striker Jay-Roy Grot from Dutch Jupiler League side NEC Nijmegen for an undisclosed fee in the summer of 2017. The exciting 19-year-old joined the club on a four-year deal, keeping him at Elland Road until the end of the 2020/21 season. The 6ft 4in centre forward, who can also operate as a winger, featured 24 times in all competitions for NEC last season, netting six goals. Grot made his debut at NEC in 2015 and despite his age, has already made 30 appearances in the Dutch top flight, the Eredivisie.

KEMAR ROOFE

POSITION: **FORWARD**
NATIONALITY: **ENGLISH**
DATE OF BIRTH: **06/01/1993**

Kemar Roofe signed a four-year deal upon joining the Whites from Oxford United in the summer of 2016. Roofe, a former West Brom trainee, established himself as one of the Football League's hottest properties during 2015/16 as he helped fire his side to promotion to League One with 26 goals from 49 appearances and his peformances earned him the League Two Player of the Year Award. The versatile attacker, who played alongside fellow United forward Chris Wood during his time in West Brom's youth system, has previously spent time on loan at Icelandic side Vikingur Reykjavik, as well as homeland clubs Northampton Town, Cheltenham Town and Colchester United.

EOGHAN STOKES

POSITION: **FORWARD**
NATIONALITY: **IRISH**
DATE OF BIRTH: **17/05/1996**

Another product of the Leeds United Academy, forward Eoghan Stokes was a regular scorer for the Under-23s during the 2016/17 campaign. Stokes was handed his senior United debut in August 2017 and led the Whites' attack against League Two outfit Newport County in the second round of the Carabao Cup, with Leeds running out 5-1 winners at Elland Road. The forward has also represented the Republic of Ireland at youth level, making appearances for their Under-17s and Under-19s. Following his debut, Stokes will be hoping to earn further minutes on the pitch throughout the 2017/18 campaign.

PHENOMENAL SUPPORT

LEEDS UNITED'S SUPPORT IS INCREDIBLE BOTH AT HOME AND AWAY, CREATING SOME OF THE BEST ATMOSPHERES IN THE COUNTRY. HERE WE TAKE A LOOK AT THEM IN ACTION!

Logistics
32Red 32Red 32Red 32Red 32Red
SKY BET SKY BET
Clipper Clipper

MEET THE BOSS

THOMAS CHRISTIANSEN WAS APPOINTED SUCCESSOR TO GARRY MONK AS LEEDS UNITED HEAD COACH ON THE 15TH JUNE 2017.

Christiansen arrived at Elland Road from APOEL Nicosia in Cyprus after winning the First Division title in the 2016/17 season and having previously led APOEL to the last 16 of the UEFA Europa League.

Prior to his spell at APOEL, the 44-year-old secured AEK Larnaca two second place finishes in the Cypriot First Division, the highest position in the club's history.

Born in Denmark, as a player Christiansen started his career with Barcelona and also had spells at Villarreal and German outfit VfL Bochum.

With VfL Bochum he was the top goal-scorer in the Bundesliga during the 2002/03 season.

With the option to play for Denmark or Spain at international level, he opted for the latter, winning two caps for Spain and scoring one goal.

Upon arriving Christiansen said: "I'm very excited and happy to have this opportunity, to come to a big club like Leeds United.

THOMAS CHRISTIANSEN

DATE OF BIRTH: 11/03/1973

BIRTHPLACE: HADSUND, DENMARK

PLAYING CAREER: BARCELONA, SPORTING GIJÓN, OSASUNA, RACING SANTANDER, OVIEDO, VILLARREAL, TERRASSA, PANIONIOS, HERFØLGE, VFL BOCHUM, HANNOVER 96.

PLAYING POSITION: STRIKER

TEAMS MANAGED: AEK LARNACA, APOEL, LEEDS UNITED

TWITTER: @T9CHRISTIANSEN

"It has a great deal of history and fantastic supporters, all the information I received about the club was really positive.

"I've always wanted to work in England, when I was a child I used to see English football constantly, coming from Denmark, this is what I grew up with.

"The atmosphere at the club is very good, the stadium is amazing.

"I've analysed a lot of the games from last season and I know the potential of the players and the club. "I am here because I want to do great things with the squad and the club, I can't speak about what we will achieve, but I can assure everyone we will work very hard.

"I know there will be pressure from the fans, but I put pressure on myself. I have just come from a club in APOEL who are expected to win every week, so the pressure isn't a problem.

"The Championship is a very difficult league, there are big teams who will have the same targets as we have, so we know it will be tough.

"I want the supporters to be close to the team, they are very passionate and very strong, we all need to be together.

"Team spirit is very important to me, the players are everything at any club. You have to have a winning mentality, you have to be ambitious to reach your goals and the players have to learn.

"It is a big step to come to English football and join a club like Leeds, who finished in seventh position in the last campaign. I think Leeds deserved to finish in a better position, but we have to work hard to ensure we reach our goals.

"With the help of everyone and the support of the fans, we can make this season a good season."

UNITED IN AUSTRIA

After taking on Harrogate Town, Guiseley and North Ferriby United, preparations for the 2017/18 campaign continued with a ten-day stay in Austria where the Whites came up against opposition from across Europe. Along with valuable training and game time, there was a vital period of team bonding with Thomas Christiansen's summer arrivals.

TRAINING

The squad spent ten days in Austria, staying just outside of Jenbach and training at the Donau Arena. Thomas Christiansen put his side through their paces with double sessions throughout their stay at the Donau Arena, with a variety of practices in order for his side to be ready ahead of the new season. The squad were also able utilise the gym and pool facilities within the team hotel in order to be in peak physical condition ahead of August's Sky Bet Championship opener against Bolton Wanderers.

Head coach Thomas Christiansen explained: "It is important to come away and be with the team together. Having the opportunity to work in a closed environment, where everyone is focused on the same thing is really beneficial. We will all get to know each other better and the tour is a great way for the players to understand what I want and of course we have games here against decent opponents."

16
9

AVIA

32Red
- Projektentwic

TEAM BONDING

Pre-season tours are always great for team bonding and United's summer trip to Austria was no different as the whole squad and backroom team went white water rafting.

On eight rafts, everyone headed off down the river.

Thomas Christiansen said: "We took the afternoon off and did some team building with the squad after the big effort they put in throughout the tour.

"The training had been tough, we had an intense session before the white water rafting, so we wanted to do something a bit different to bond during this activity."

Speaking about the experience, defender Luke Ayling added: "It was really good, the whole team got to experience it together, there were lots of laughs and jokes, the water was very cold though. All of the boys joined in and it was a great afternoon."

MEETING SUPPORTERS

Midway through United's tour of Austria, supporters were invited by head coach Thomas Christiansen to attend an open training session. The Whites fans who made the trip to Europe were able to see exactly how the team were put through their paces ahead of the campaign. Following the training session, supporters were given the opportunity to meet and have photos with their favourite United stars.

MATCHES

Two friendly matches and a training game took place in Austria, with Thomas Christiansen's side coming away with a draw and two defeats.

After United's first pre-season game against FC Ingolstadt 04 was cancelled at 48 hours notice, the Whites arranged a last minute, behind closed doors training game against Bursaspor in Italy and were defeated 3-0.

Second up were German Bundesliga outfit Borussia Mönchengladbach, which took place at Schwaz. Full-back Luke Ayling gave United an early lead inside two minutes, but that goal was cancelled out in the second-half, with Patrick Herrmann netting a free-kick two minutes after the break.

United then took on SD Eibar at their training base, the Donau Arena, in the final match of the tour, but were defeated 4-2. After trailing 3-0 at half time, Chris Wood and Ezgjan Alioski gave Leeds hope, however a late effort from Paulo Oliveira secured the Spanish La Liga outfit the victory.

The Whites then played their final game at Elland Road, with Leeds coming up against former assistant manager Pep Clotet's Oxford United. Goals from Kemar Roofe and Stuart Dallas, ensured Leeds would start the season on the back of a friendly victory.

RONALDO VIEIRA

2017/18 KIT LAUNCH

Our 2017/18 home kit was unveiled at an exclusive Elland Road event for Season Ticket Holders back in the summer, with Gaetano Berardi, Pontus Jansson, Kemar Roofe, Marcus Antonsson, Mateusz Klich, Rob Green, Liam Cooper and Ronaldo Vieira all on hand to model the new white and gold kit. The players were also joined by a selection of lucky Junior Season Ticket Holders who proudly displayed the Utilita Energy logo on their shirt, after an opening Q&A session with Thomas Christiansen. Our club photographer captured all of the action!

THE BIG LEEDS UNITED QUIZ

1 What colour is the Leeds 2017/18 away kit?

2 What squad number does Luke Ayling wear for Leeds?

3 According to the football chant, what does Pontus Jansson wear?

4 Which stand is the biggest at Elland Road?

5 What position does Eunan O'Kane play?

6 In what year did Leeds United sign Stuart Dallas?

7 How many goals did Pablo Hernández score last season?

8 What nationality is goalkeeper Felix Wiedwald?

9 Vurnon Anita joined Leeds from which club?

10 True or false: Ezgjan Alioski plays for Macedonia?

11 What position did Leeds United finish in the Sky Bet Championship in the 2016/17 season?

12 Who won Leeds United's Player of the Year Award in 2017?

13 What nationality is winger Hadi Sacko?

14 Mateusz Klich joined Leeds United from which club?

15 True or false: Head Coach Thomas Christiansen once played for Barcelona?

16 Who is Leeds United's record goal-scorer?

17 The West Stand at Elland Road is named after which former player?

18 In what year did Leeds United last win the FA Cup?

19 In what year was Leeds United founded?

20 How many times have Leeds United won the First Division (now Premier League)?

SPOT THE DIFFERENCE

Answers on page 60

CAN YOU SPOT THE SIX DIFFERENCES IN THIS PHOTO OF SAMUEL SAIZ AGAINST PRESTON NORTH END?

32Red
21
Kappa
2Red

WORDSEARCH

FIND THE WORDS IN THE GRID. WORDS CAN GO HORIZONTALLY, VERTICALLY AND DIAGONALLY IN ALL EIGHT DIRECTIONS.

J	D	L	A	W	D	E	I	W	J
A	L	N	R	K	M	R	N	P	I
N	L	F	Z	I	A	S	P	H	K
S	B	E	R	A	R	D	I	I	S
S	N	C	T	C	G	R	T	L	O
O	W	D	O	N	O	H	W	L	I
N	L	P	I	O	W	C	J	I	L
H	R	L	F	V	P	L	L	P	A
C	Y	E	K	B	N	E	M	S	N
A	R	I	E	I	V	C	R	K	K

ALIOSKI
AYLING
BERARDI
COOPER
JANSSON
PHILLIPS
ROOFE
SAIZ
VIEIRA
WIEDWALD

Answers on page 60

32Red
19
Kappa
LUFC
LUFC

RONALDO VIEIRA-FANTASY 6-A-SIDE

LEEDS UNITED MIDFIELDER RONALDO VIEIRA PICKS HIS FANTASY 6-A-SIDE TEAM. RULES APPLY THOUGH – HE MUST HAVE PLAYED WITH THREE OF THE PLAYERS INCLUDED IN HIS TEAM.

MARCO SILVESTRI

The goalkeeper started his career at Chievo Verona before being snapped up by Leeds United in 2014. He spent three years with the Whites, before moving to Hellas Verona in the summer of 2017.

RENATO SANCHES

Coming through the ranks at Benfica, Sanches moved to Bayern Munich in 2016. He is regarded as one of the best midfielders in the world and helped Portugal win Euro 2016.

THIAGO SILVA

The Brazilian defender has won league titles in both Italy and Spain and is regarded as one of the best defenders in the world. He has been at Paris Saint-Germain since 2012 and has over 60 caps for Brazil.

ARJEN ROBBEN

Known for his lightning pace, Robben has played for some of the biggest clubs in the world including Real Madrid and Bayern Munich. He has won league titles in the Netherlands, England, Spain and Germany and played in a World Cup final.

PABLO HERNÁNDEZ

Spanish midfielder Pablo Hernández began his career at Valencia and also had a spell at Getafe, before joining Swansea City in 2012. A move to Qatar followed, before joining Leeds, where he is a key player for the Whites. He has won four caps for Spain, scoring one goal.

RONALDO

The now-retired Brazilian striker was one of the greatest ever players to grace a football pitch. Playing for Barcelona, Real Madrid, Inter Milan and AC Milan, he was a prolific goal scorer and won two FIFA World Cups with Brazil.

Kappa
32Red
2Red
Kappa
32Re

CROSSWORD

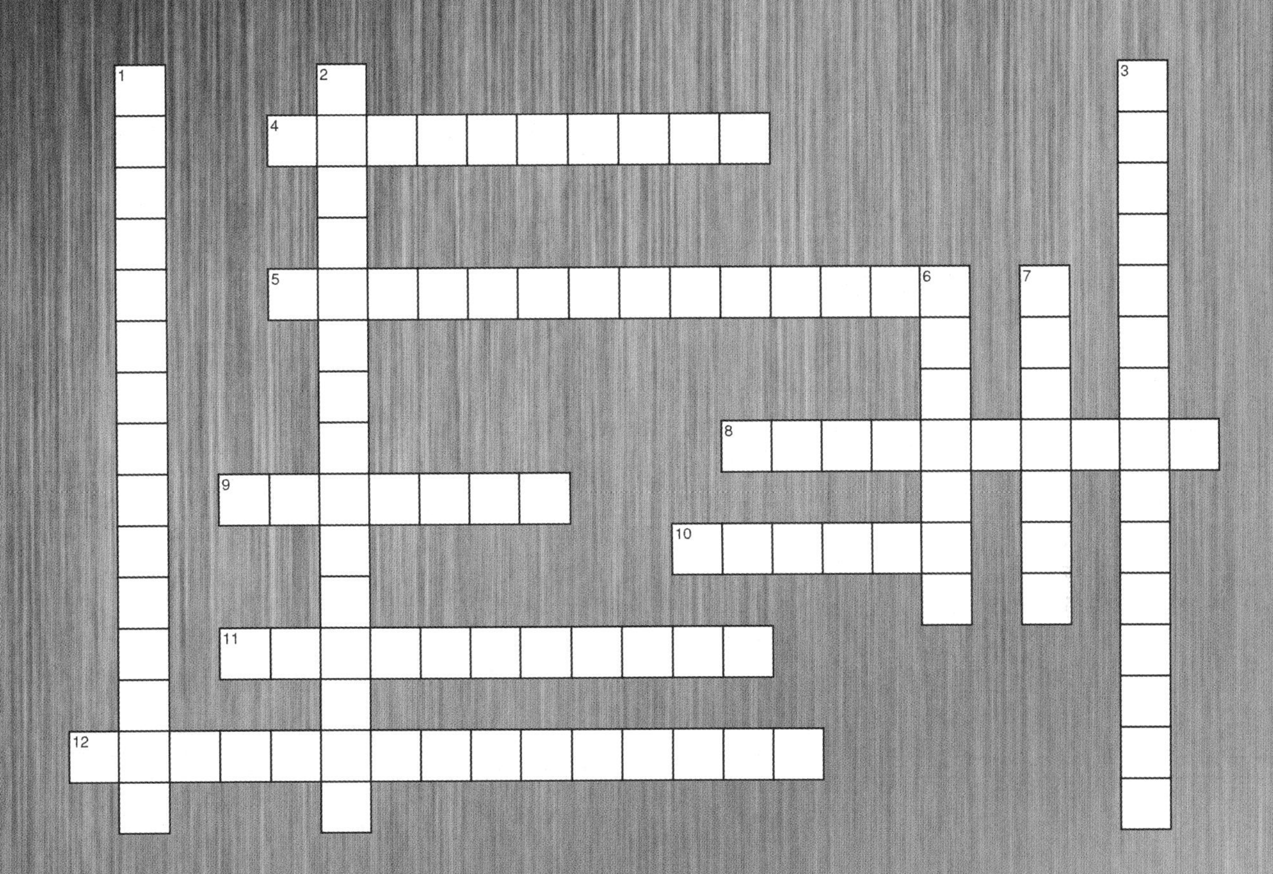

ACROSS

4 Who wears shirt number 7 for Leeds United? (5,5)

5 Who wears shirt number 23 for Leeds United? (6,8)

8 What is the name of our home ground? (6,4)

9 What nationality is Pontus Jansson? (7)

10 In which country did Thomas Christiansen manage before joining Leeds United? (6,8)

11 Which club did Leeds United sign Luke Ayling from? (7,3)

12 Which country does Stuart Dallas play international football for? (7,7)

DOWN

1 Which manager guided Leeds United to the First Division title in the 1991/92 season? (6,9)

2 Which club did Leeds United sign Vurnon Anita from? (9,6)

3 Who did Leeds United play in the first game of the 2017/18 Sky Bet Championship season? (6,8)

6 What nationality is Pablo Hernandez? (7)

7 Matthew Pennington joined Leeds United on loan from which club? (7)

Answers on page 61

ASK PONTUS JANSSON

@alexcasss asked: ABBA or IKEA?
Pontus: "I have to say IKEA, because when I lived in Italy I bought a lot of furniture there and since being here in Leeds too. Of course ABBA are massive and I'm proud they're from Sweden."

@LUFCDATA asked: Which centre-back has made the biggest impression on your career?
Pontus: "I was always a striker as a kid, I always liked to dribble, score goals and do crazy things with the ball. I watched a lot of strikers, like Zlatan Ibrahimovic, of course, because he is from Sweden. If I had to choose a defender, I would say Thiago Silva, he played a lot with Zlatan at Paris and I've watched him a lot, he is very good."

@PatrickProcter asked: Who is the most difficult striker you came up against in your first campaign in England?
Pontus: "It is a difficult question, you'd have to say someone who scored against us. Probably Dwight Gayle for Newcastle, he scored twice, despite not arguably having the best game against us, he is a good player."

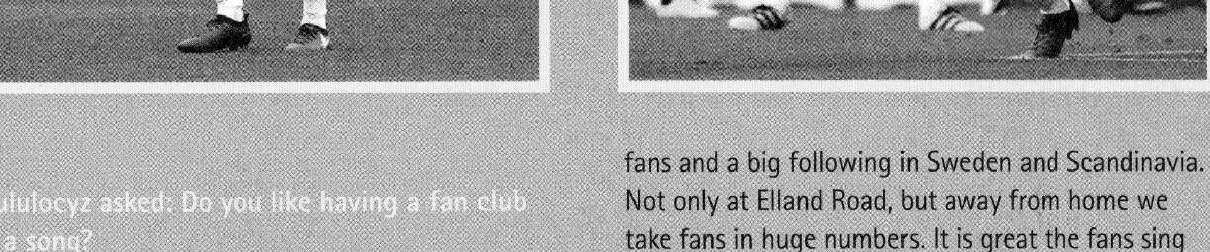

@Lululocyz asked: Do you like having a fan club and a song?
Pontus: "Of course! I am really thankful for it, when everyone sings my song it makes me really happy. I am also very thankful for having a fan club and I really like it."

@lwhiteleyl asked: What made you want to become a defender?
Pontus: "When I was 18 or 19, I was at Malmö with our former assistant head coach Pep Clotet. At the club we had five or six strikers and it was a tough situation for me. There were only two or three defenders and I was asked if I would play in defence. I agreed because I was thinking about the team and two or three games into the season, our regular defender got injured and after that I played for the rest of the campaign and we won the league."

@ingham37 asked: Do you like Yorkshire Puddings with gravy, by themselves or as part of a meal?
Pontus: "I've actually never eaten a Yorkshire Pudding, but I have heard a lot about it. I haven't tried it yet, but I will have to do it soon, so I can answer this question!"

@Lambo1903 asked: What is it like playing in front of the Leeds fans every week?
Pontus: "It is a special feeling. Leeds is a big club and I knew that before I came here. Leeds have great fans and a big following in Sweden and Scandinavia. Not only at Elland Road, but away from home we take fans in huge numbers. It is great the fans sing and back us in every game and we are all thankful for that."

@TonyDickinson asked: What is your favourite music?
Pontus: "My favourite music is Swedish hip-hop and I always prepare for the games with that."

@BazingaCJ asked: You've scored for Leeds against Aston Villa, Blackburn Rovers and Norwich City – which was your favourite goal?
Pontus: "Norwich was great because it was my first goal and I jumped into the crowd to celebrate with the fans! Aston Villa is a big club and it was an important goal to score there too. But it has to be Blackburn, out of the three. We had 6,000-7,000 away fans there and the goal was scored in the last minute to win the game. Of course, every goal is special."

@PunknDrunken asked: If the whole season came down to penalties at the end of the season, would you step up and take one?
"Like I said, I was a striker when I was younger and of course somewhere inside of me is a goal-scorer. I am not a nervous type of player, so I would step up, but it would be up to the coach."

YOU ARE THE GAFFER
LUKE AYLING

Tracksuit or suit? Suit

Formation of choice? 3-5-2

Zonal or man marking? A mixture of both.

What style would your team play?
Get it up-field, nice and early and play in their half, with a high press.

Which manager would you be most like?
José Mourinho, I'd be a man manager.

You are playing your main rivals, do you talk them up or play it down?
Play it down, normal game, go out there and play your football.

What fine would you introduce?
No hats or jewellery and no headphones when you get off the coach, so everyone looks the same.

What team bonding activity would you chose?
Drinking

You are in the Premier League – would you prefer Champions League qualification or winning the FA Cup?
I think now it's all about the top four, it's great to win a trophy but everyone wants to play in the Champions League (I mean obviously I've played it, so I know what it takes to be there, I've done it, so I know what it takes).

You can sign any goalkeeper, defender, midfielder and striker in the world, who are they?
Manuel Neuer, Kyle Bartley (he's perfect in every sense), Luka Modric and Lionel Messi.

32Red

LIAM COOPER

SPOT THE BALL

Answers on page 61

GOING FOR GOAL

STUART DALLAS, CALEB EKUBAN AND SAMUEL SAIZ ARE ALL TRYING TO SCORE, BUT ONLY ONE OF THEM CAN COMPLETE THE TASK - CAN YOU WORK OUT WHO WILL FIND THE NET?

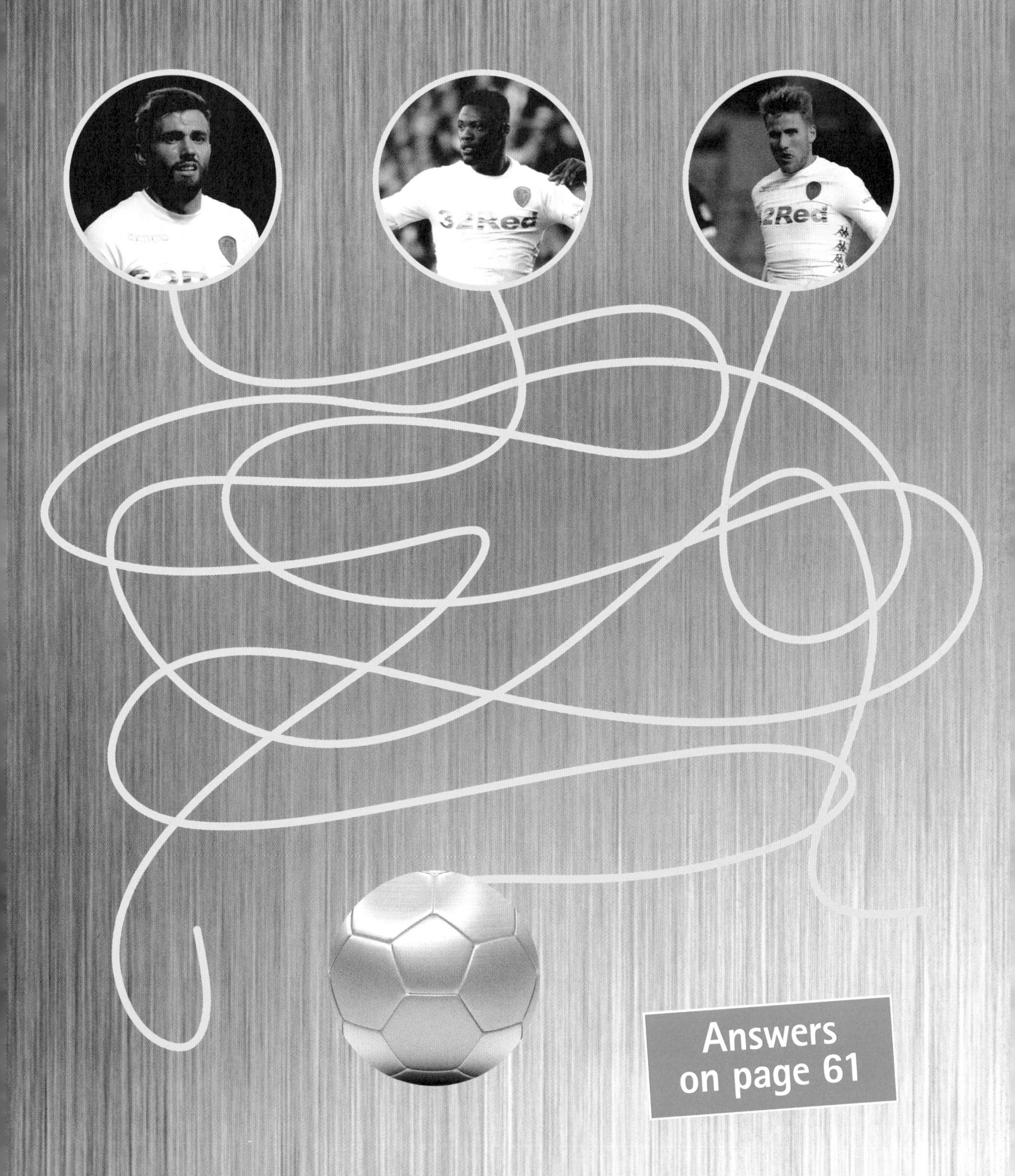

Answers on page 61

GAETANO BERARDI

CLUB FACTS AND FIGURES

Nicknames: 'United' or 'The Whites'

First choice colours: White with blue and gold trim

Change colours: All black

Leeds United came into being late in 1919 but it was 1920 when the club gained election to the Football League.

Record attendance: 57,892 v Sunderland FA Cup 5th rnd replay March 15 1967

Record League win: 8-0 v Leicester City, Division One, April 7 1934

Record European win: 10-0 v Lyn Oslo, European Cup 1st rnd 1st leg September 17 1969

Record FA Cup win: 8-1 v Crystal Palace (Rnd 3) January 1930

FIRST GAME IN FOOTBALL LEAGUE: AUGUST 28 1920, DIVISION TWO V PORT VALE (A) LOST 0-2

Record League Cup win: 5-1 v Mansfield Town (Rnd 2), September 1963

Record League defeat: 1-8 v Stoke City, Division One, August 27 1934

Record European defeat: 0-4 v SK Lierse (UEFA Cup) 1st rnd, 1st leg, Sept 1971 / Barcelona (Champs League), Sept 2000

Record FA Cup defeat: 2-7 v Middlesbrough (Rnd 3), January 1946

MATCH SEQUENCES

Unbeaten start to the season: 29 (1973/74)

Most successive wins in all competitions to start season: 8 (2009/10)

Longest undefeated run: 34 (Oct 1968 – Aug 1969)

Longest undefeated run at home: 39 (May 1968 – March 1970)

Longest undefeated run away: 17 (Oct 1968 – Aug 1969)

Successive home wins (league): 15 (Jan 2009 – Oct 2010)

Successive defeats (league): 6 (April 1947 – May 1947)

Successive games without a win (league): 17 (January 1947 – August 1947)

Longest run without a home win: 10 (February 1982 – May 1982)

Longest run without an away win: 26 (March 1939 – August 1947)

Record League Cup defeat: 0-7 v West Ham (Rnd 3), November 1966 / Arsenal (Rnd 2), September 1979

Record League scorer in a season: John Charles 43, Division Two 1953 - 54

Highest number of league goals in a match: 5, Gordon Hodgson v Leicester City, Division One, October 1 1938

Highest number of League goals in aggregate: Peter Lorimer 168

Record all-time goalscorer: Peter Lorimer 238

Record appearances in league matches: Jack Charlton 629

Record all-time appearances: 773 Jack Charlton / Billy Bremner

Record transfer fee paid: £18m to West Ham for Rio Ferdinand, November 2000

Record transfer fee received: £29.1m from Manchester Utd for Rio Ferdinand, July 2002

37,890

ELLAND ROAD CAPACITY

Oldest Player: Eddie Burbank (41yrs and 23 days) – v Hull City, April 1954

Youngest Player: Peter Lorimer (15 years and 289 days) – v Southampton, September 1962

First schoolboy to play for club: Tom Elliott v Norwich City, February 3, 2007

Most players used in a season: 44 (2004/05 and 2006/07)

115 X 74 YARDS

ELLAND ROAD PITCH MEASUREMENTS

MANAGERS

Dick Ray 1919 - 1920
Arthur Fairclough 1920 - 1927
Dick Ray 1927 - 1935
Billy Hampson 1935 - 1947
Willis Edwards 1947 - 1948
Major Frank Buckley 1948 - 1953
Raich Carter 1953 - 1958
Bill Lambton 1958 - 1959
Jack Taylor 1959 - 1961
Don Revie 1961 - 1974
Brian Clough 1974
Jimmy Armfield 1974 - 1978
Jock Stein 1978 (Aug - Sept)
Jimmy Adamson 1978 - 1980
Allan Clarke 1980 - 1982
Eddie Gray 1982 - 1985
Billy Bremner 1985 - 1988
Howard Wilkinson 1988 - 1996
George Graham 1996 - 1998
David O'Leary 1998 - 2002
Terry Venables 2002 - 2003
Peter Reid 2003 (Mar - Nov)
Eddie Gray 2003 - 2004
Kevin Blackwell 2004 - 2006
Dennis Wise 2006 - 2008
Gary McAllister 2008 (Jan - Dec)
Simon Grayson 2008 - 2012
Neil Warnock 2012 - 2013
Brian McDermott 2013 - 2014
David Hockaday 2014 (June - Aug)
Darko Milanic 2014 (Sept - Oct)
Neil Redfearn 2014 - 2015
Uwe Rosler 2015 (May - Oct)
Steve Evans 2015 - 2016
Garry Monk 2016 - 2017
Thomas Christiansen 2017 -

P38: THE BIG LEEDS UNITED QUIZ

1) Black
2) 2
3) A magic hat
4) East Stand
5) Midfield
6) 2015
7) 6
8) German
9) Newcastle United
10) True
11) Seventh
12) Chris Wood
13) French
14) FC Twente
15) True
16) Peter Lorimer
17) John Charles
18) 1972
19) 1919
20) 3

P42: WORDSEARCH

J	D	L	A	W	D	E	I	W	J
A	L	N	R	K	M	R	N	P	I
N	L	F	Z	I	A	S	P	H	K
S	B	E	R	A	R	D	I	I	S
S	N	C	T	C	G	R	T	L	O
O	W	D	O	N	O	H	W	L	I
N	L	P	I	O	W	C	J	I	L
H	R	L	F	V	P	L	L	P	A
C	Y	E	K	B	N	E	M	S	N
A	R	I	E	I	V	C	R	K	K

P40: SPOT THE DIFFERENCE

P47: CROSSWORD

	H				N																B	
	O			K	E	M	A	R	R	O	O	F	E								O	
	W				W																L	
	A				C																T	
	R			K	A	L	V	I	N	P	H	I	L	L	I	P	S		E		O	
	D				S												P		V		N	
	W				T												A		E		W	
	I				L								E	L	L	A	N	D	R	O	A	D
	L		S	W	E	D	I	S	H								I		T		N	
	K				U							C	Y	P	R	U	S		O		D	
	I				N												H		N		E	
	N		B	R	I	S	T	O	L	C	I	T	Y								R	
	S				T																E	
N	O	R	T	H	E	R	N	I	R	E	L	A	N	D							R	
	N				D																S	

P53: SPOT THE BALL

Answer: A

P55: GOING FOR GOAL

Answer: Dallas

CAN YOU SPOT LUCAS WITHIN THE CROWD OF LEEDS UNITED SUPPORTERS AT ELLAND ROAD?